CHARNWOOD
FOREST
IN OLD PHOTOGRAPHS

DEDICATION

For those who love Charnwood Forest and are privileged to enjoy its many splendours.

THE EARLIEST KNOWN BRITISH FOSSIL, *Charnia masoni*, is over seven hundred million years old. This oldest known animal on earth, from the Metazoan Age, was discovered by a schoolboy in Charnwood Forest in 1958.

CHARNWOOD
FOREST
IN OLD PHOTOGRAPHS

COLLECTED BY
IAN KEIL, WALLACE HUMPHREY
& DON WIX

ALAN SUTTON
LEICESTERSHIRE MUSEUMS, ARTS AND RECORDS SERVICE.

Alan Sutton Publishing Limited
Phoenix Mill · Far Thrupp · Stroud · Gloucestershire

in association with
LEICESTERSHIRE MUSEUMS, ARTS & RECORDS SERVICE 1991

First published 1991

British Library Cataloguing in Publication Data

Charnwood Forest in old photographs.
I. Keil, Ian, *1933–*
II. Humphrey, Wallace, *1921–* III. Wix, Don
942.547

ISBN 0-7509-0068-7

Typeset in 9/10 Korinna.
Typesetting and origination by
Alan Sutton Publishing Limited.
Printed in Great Britain by
The Bath Press Avon.

CONTENTS

INTRODUCTION   6

1. MAPS AND PLACE NAMES   9

2. VILLAGE LIFE   15

3. HALLS AND HOUSES   35

4. MAKING A LIVING   59

5. RELIGIOUS LIFE   75

6. GETTING ABOUT   103

7. RESERVOIRS   115

8. MINES AND QUARRIES   123

9. ENJOYMENT   135

    ACKNOWLEDGEMENTS   160

INTRODUCTION

The intention of this selection is to share with the reader the authors' pleasure in studying a rich landscape and the people who have helped to shape it. The surviving and available pictorial evidence offers an immediate if partial view of the history of Charnwood Forest.

Our first task was to define what we believed Charnwood Forest to be. Unlike many of the ancient areas of forest in England, Charnwood in the Middle Ages was never subject to Forest Law, a legal system that required precise boundaries. We decided to include all places that at different times in the past are reputed to have formed the limits of the forest. Moreover, Charnwood covers a greater area than the district subject to the Act for the Enclosure of Charnwood Forest of 1808 or the present area designated by the Leicestershire County Council planners during the twentieth century. Another and very different area is the Borough of Charnwood, a second tier local authority that includes within its boundaries only a third of the planner's definition of the Forest.

Charnwood Forest had contracted by the time of the Enclosure Act because various landowners had already taken land from the 'waste' for deer parks or agricultural uses. By the 1920s the County planners identified Charnwood as 'villages and rural areas of great beauty that formed a core for careful protection from unsightly development but accessible to the growing populations of the towns within easy reach.' Their maps show the Forest enclosed by the Act and the district now accepted as Charnwood Forest for planning purposes.

The complex geological structure of Charnwood Forest owes much to ancient volcanic activity and earth movements. It covers within a comparatively small area some hard granite rocks, slate and, on its western margin, coal measures. The soils differ in depth and fertility according to location and long-term action of wind and climate. A few woodlands have had a continuous existence from prehistoric times. Thin soils have made some parts fit only for pastures since time immemorial.

Before the nineteenth century most people living in Charnwood Forest depended on the resources of their own locality for their livelihood and few villages had populations numbering more than a thousand people. Agriculture formed an important part of the economy, with grain crops grown on the better soils. On the lusher pastures farmers kept a few cattle for local consumption and oxen and horses were the draught animals. The greater part of the grasslands supported sheep. Parks created by wealthy landowners in the twelfth or thirteenth centuries as prestigious hunting reservations had mostly given way to animal husbandry or decorative parkland surroundings for great houses. Charnwood Forest had some areas that were too poor for agriculture and this waste gave some sanctuary to wildlife. Extensive woodland within the Forest had diminished as timber demands for both building purposes and fuel grew. The latter need had led to much felling in the second half of the seventeenth century, with the development of smelting in the iron industry in Whitwick and Melbourne. Such cleared land reverted to waste or became farmland according to its quality.

In 1828 the commissioners appointed under the 1808 Charnwood Forest Enclosure Act divided the land covered by the law among those who had ownership rights. This changed the face of the countryside: new roads cut straight across the land, boundaries were drawn with geometrical precision and hedges and fences created regular fields. This transformation was accompanied by investment in building farmhouses and restocking farms. Agriculture experienced differing fortunes both locally and nationally. Its decline as a source of revenue and employment in the last quarter of the nineteenth century was accentuated by the areas of poor soil that were no longer worth working intensively. In some cases these areas became woodland. The revival of agriculture after the beginning of the Second World War brought investment in farming, including mechanization, and the changes in the agricultural policies of the European Community during the later 1970s have encouraged the cultivation of new crops such as rapeseed and some new uses of land.

Employment in quarrying for stone and coal has origins in the distant past. Until the advent of cheap long-distance transport, stone was carried by horse and wagon for use within about fifteen miles of quarries. Thus we find Swithland slate used for gravestones in much of Leicestershire, and this slate also provided good roofing tiles. Slate ceased to be quarried by the end of the nineteenth century because of competition from cheaper products from Wales or overseas. The hard granite was exploited as improved roads in towns and on major routes became necessary during the nineteenth century. The canals and, later, the railways expanded the markets for Leicestershire products in the latter part of the twentieth century. More than a third of the roadstone used in the United Kingdom comes from Charnwood's quarries. The coal mined at the western end of the Forest came from the West Leicestershire coalfield which ceased production by deep-mining methods in the late 1980s. Small deposits of other minerals have been worked, such as honing stone from Whittle Hill and lead ore from near Shepshed.

The natural drainage has been harnessed since the mid-nineteenth century to fill reservoirs supplying the towns of Leicester, Loughborough and Shepshed. Populations not only grew in size but their improved domestic life styles and their industries required ever greater water supplies.

The economy of Charnwood Forest has depended upon its transport facilities. Its road network was mainly the result of the early nineteenth century changes brought about by the Enclosures. During the twentieth century the principal route innovation has been the building of the M1 during the mid-1960s. On the northern periphery of the Forest the Charnwood Canal ran from Nanpantan to the north-west Leicestershire coalfield for only a short time, but remains of the canal still exist. More significant was the canalization of the River Soar that served the eastern edges of the Forest, particularly at Quorn and Mountsorrel. The Forest had no railway passing through it until the building of the Charnwood Forest Railway during the early 1880s. It followed part of the disused canal dug almost a century earlier. This railway served Loughborough and Coalville. The line closed even before the Beeching axe of 1963 closed many branch lines. The last main line to be built in England, the Great Central, was conceived as a means of linking Manchester with Paris via a Channel Tunnel. It was carved through the Forest in the 1890s.

The number of jobs within the Charnwood Forest area declined from the middle of the nineteenth century. Mechanization swept away most of the domestic productions of hosiery and lace. Agriculture employed fewer and fewer people. Mining and quarrying likewise became more mechanized. Only trades associated with tourism sustained or increased their numbers. Most of the income of Forest dwellers comes from commuting to large towns. This transformation of the social structure of towns and villages within the area began with the frequent rail services of the beginning of the twentieth century but was augmented by regular bus services. During the past half century, when the greatest increase in commuting occurred, private motor cars have so altered the life of villages that some have very few shops.

The distinctive religious and educational life of Charnwood Forest has left many reminders. After the Norman conquest, benefactors gave marginal lands to Augustinians, Cistercians, Knights Templar and a few hermits. The Templars were replaced by the Knights of St John of Jerusalem. All these regular religious organizations disappeared at the Reformation. 'The Second Spring' of Roman Catholicism was marked by the establishment of the Cistercian house at Mount St Bernard's Abbey in 1834. The growth of population within the Charnwood Forest area from the middle of the eighteenth century encouraged missionary efforts – the Church of England created new parishes, and other Christian denominations built churches and chapels to serve their adherents.

Commuters and tourists are successors to the more limited number of people who were able to enjoy Charnwood Forest in the past. Alongside the visual and sensual pleasures of the forest, hunting and fishing still continue. New uses of land since the latter part of the nineteenth century have included golf, bird-watching, rambling or more formal entertainments in Bradgate Park. More people with more leisure have seen Charnwood as a source of delight. The onus remains on us to safeguard the rich flora and fauna for our successors.

Maps and Place Names

THE TRIGONOMETRICAL POINT at 818 ft (249 m) on top of Beacon Hill was used as a marker for accurate map-making. On a clear day landmarks not far distant from the Wash may be seen.

JOANNES JANSSONIUS OF AMSTERDAM published his map of Leicestershire in 1654. This extract shows the outer limits of the area associated with Charnwood Forest. Symbolic trees beside 'Charnwood Forest' represent neither its extent at this period nor the extent of the wooded area. Places with forest rights included Belton and Shepshed in the north, Groby and Thurcaston in the south, Thornton and Donington-le-Heath in the west and Quorn and Rothley in the east.

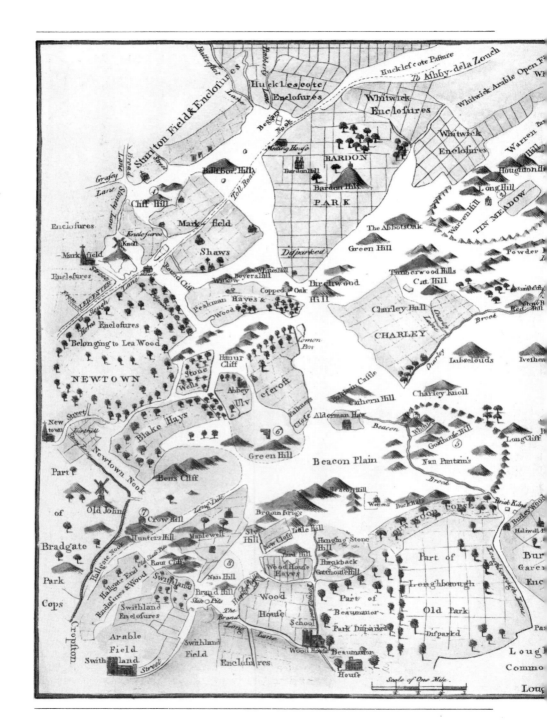

JOHN NICHOLS PUBLISHED THIS MAP, which has the west instead of the north at the top, but it covered only some of the area of forest. The map had been drawn in the eighteenth century to show the heartland of Charnwood with the parks belonging to the landed families. Even Bradgate Park crept into the map at the bottom. Many of the indicated features have survived.

ANSTEY: settlement with a high footpath.

BELTON: 'ton' means a farmstead; 'bel' is obscure.

BENSCLIFFE: uncertain meaning; usually 'ben' means bean.

BRADGATE: the wide path.

CHARLEY: woodland where there are rocks.

CHARNWOOD: the name appeared in 1276 as 'Charnewode'. 'Charne' means rocky or stony. Although 'wode' meant woodland, the area was never legally a forest, this being the term to describe a royal hunting park, closed to the general public and often the cause of much annoyance. Wooded areas used for sport by subjects of the crown were known as 'chases' if they were large. For example, Cannock Chase in Staffordshire was a hunting ground of the Bishops of Lichfield. Charnwood is occasionally quoted as a chase but the courtesy title 'forest' is usually applied to it. Areas smaller than chases were called parks and were used by the local nobility. An example within Charnwood was Bradgate. Two parks just outside Charnwood were Loughborough and Burley, either side of the modern Nanpantan Road.

COALVILLE: a settlement where there is coal, a nineteenth-century name.

COPT OAK: possibly a place with a very tall tree. The Old English 'copp' means 'with a top'.

CROPSTON: Cropp's 'tun'. 'Tun' was a settlement (now spelt 'town' or 'ton').

GARENDON: Gaerwald's don; a personal name followed by 'don' meaning hill.

GRACEDIEU: God's Grace; there was a nunnery here.

GROBY: debatable meaning; suggestions include 'torrent' or 'hollow'. The 'by' ending is Scandinavian for a settlement.

IVESHEAD: a possible meaning is 'steep hill'.

MARKFIELD: the open land of the Mercians.

MOUNTSORREL: the mount or hill has been respectively the site of a castle and windmill for centuries.

NANPANTAN: the name first appears on a map dated 1754 (see pp. 12, 13) as 'Nan Pantain's near the Outwoods'. The nature of the lady's establishment is unknown.

NEWTOWN LINFORD: the settlement was developed when existing land became overworked. The name means 'new town on the ford where there are lime trees'.

QUORNDON: the village has only recently become Quorn. Quorndon was a hill where querns were found. A quern was a millstone so the area referred to is probably granite.

ROTHLEY: an open space by a stream by a clearing.

SHEPSHED: a hill where sheep were grazed. (This may refer to Iveshead.)

SWITHLAND: land cleared by burning, a method sometimes used to open up wooded areas.

THRINGSTONE: a Danish settlement whose 'by' ending had changed to 'ton' by about 1200. 'Thring' may mean land that was difficult to work.

ULVERSCROFT: where Ulf farmed his croft (farmland).

WHITWICK: 'wic' is derived from the old English word for dairy farm. 'Whit' means white or dairy farm.

WOODHOUSE: houses in a wood.

WOODHOUSE EAVES: houses on the borders of a wood.

Village Life

MAIN STREET IN MOUNTSORREL in 1900 when it was safe to walk in the middle of the road. Horses were not so frequent as the cars of later days.

THE BULLS HEAD AT WOODHOUSE EAVES in 1919 still formed part of the Beaumanor estate and changed ownership when the estate was sold in 1946. Since this time the house has been twice modernized. Mrs Perry Herrick, an ardent teetotaller, arranged that this public house and the Curzon Arms in the village had no licence to sell alcohol on Sundays.

THE WHEATSHEAF AT THURCASTON in 1904 is typical of many village inns of the time.

THE BRADGATE ARMS in Main Street, Newtown Linford has a horse-drawn delivery van beside it, a scene probably frequently repeated in the late Victorian period. The village inn sought to broaden its appeal by an advertisement in Spencers' *Guide* in the 1890s (below). It was repeated over a number of years, implying that tourism in Charnwood was established.

THE KING WILLIAM IV AT QUORN was named after the 'sailor king' who reigned from 1830 to 1837. During the Second World War it was a favourite meeting place for the 82nd Airborne Division of the US Army. The building was demolished in 1956.

THE THREE CROWNS AT WHITWICK in the early twentieth century was just one of a variety of public houses that met the needs of a community dominated by coalmining. The street was lit by gas.

THE GRIFFIN INN AT SWITHLAND was once the Griffin Hotel, in Main Street, and offered amenities to both villagers and visitors from farther afield. The Spencers' *Guide* advertisement from the 1890s points out the newly built reservoir as an additional attraction for visitors to enjoy in the countryside.

THE PRIORY was erected at Nanpantan in the early 1920s, replacing the licensed Longcliffe Hotel on the opposite corner. It had all the facilities of the popular roadhouse, including a spacious dancehall-cum-dining-room. Roadhouses were a development by brewery firms to provide a modern atmosphere for out of town entertainment and take advantage of outings by charabancs and private cars. Local residents succeeded in restricting the licence so that dancing did not form a regular part of available entertainment. The Nineteenth Hole bar reflected the proximity of the Longcliffe golf club.

THE MIXED YEARS of St Peter's school in Mountsorrel about 1900 probably wore their Sunday best for the school photograph.

MISS REBECCA JACQUES founded a private school in Mountsorrel in 1846 and by 1897 it was run by Miss Sarah Jacques (on the left) with her sister Annie.

THIS VIEW FROM THE CASTLE HILL AT MOUNTSORREL shows in the foreground the Buttermarket Cross and the core of the village with slate or thatched roofs. The settlement was constrained on the hill side by the rapid rise in the ground and further away by the flood plain of the River Soar. The effective limits were reinforced by the canalization of the river in the 1790s so that a loop of navigation passed close to the village. This served the needs of the quarries, which had a landing stage to the right of the road that turns off the main street and leads to Sileby. The population grew rapidly during the nineteenth century, thanks to the increase in employment for workers in the stone quarries and factories. No landowner attempted to restrict newcomers so people moved in from some of the nearby Wolds villages, where few opportunities for work existed.

THE BUTTER CROSS AT MOUNTSORREL in 1890. It was erected in 1793 by the owner of Swithland Hall to replace a market cross. It provided a covered market for village produce and served as a meeting place for public occasions. The road surface was of the pre-tarmacadam type, being made of graded stones to form a camber.

THE GREEN AT MOUNTSORREL at the end of the nineteenth century is a scene now much altered, with rebuilding and encroachments upon this open space.

AN ARMISTICE PARADE by members of the British Legion held at Mountsorrel in the 1920s. The quarry forms a backdrop for this commemoration. The war memorial stands on the hill above the village.

AN EARLY TWENTIETH-CENTURY FUNERAL CORTEGE at Mountsorrel with a horse-drawn hearse. Presumably, the numerous mourners and followers show the popularity of the former resident.

ROTHLEY developed round its church and village green, having been a market centre since the Middle Ages for the nearby forest area. Its industries once included knitwear, although now most people commute from the village to work in nearby large towns.

MOST OF THE STONE-BUILT COTTAGES with slate roofs in Fowke Street, Rothley are now demolished.

MAIN STREET, SWITHLAND once had most of its roofs thatched, but costs of thatching and insurance premiums encouraged many owners to adopt Swithland slate tiles. Now the village relies on commuters living here for its existence, but until the end of the nineteenth century slate-quarrying and the domestic system of knitwear production provided the important elements for economic well-being.

THE BUS IN THE BULL RING, SHEPSHED in the late 1920s stands in front of the grandiose late Victorian building which has become the National Westminster Bank.

A BREWER'S DRAY delivering barrels to the Bull's Head at Shepshed. This scene was commonplace in the early twentieth century. To the right the booking office of the GCR (Great Central Railway) reminds us that the company disappeared in the railway amalgamations enforced by the Act of 1921 which made it part of the London & North Eastern Railway.

THE BULL RING AT SHEPSHED had a bus stop for services to Coalville, Leicester, Loughborough and neighbouring villages during the 1930s. The main services were supplied by the Midland Red Company which took over many routes after unbridled competition led to the regulation of bus traffic by the Act of 1933.

THE BULLRING AT SHEPSHED awash with flood waters early in the twentieth century.

FIREMEN ASSISTING BUILDERS to secure a waterproof cover on a thatched roof in the 1930s.

FIELD STREET, SHEPSHED was one of the main thoroughfares of the 'largest village' in Leicestershire. This scene of around 1920 shows the predominance of Victorian buildings indicating the revival of the community's fortunes after the middle of the nineteenth century. Hosiery and knitwear trades provided the largest amount of employment, but in small factories rather than as a cottage industry. Among the shops in the street was the Co-operative, established in 1866.

MAIN STREET IN WOODHOUSE EAVES during the 1930s, showing the parish church dominating the centre of the village. The development of bus services and the wider ownership of private cars transformed the village economy so that it became dependent on commuters who worked in nearby large towns.

THE VIEW FROM THE PARISH CHURCH at Woodhouse Eaves in the 1920s shows it little developed and so not encouraging new residents. Maplewell Road has only a few Victorian houses. On the open rise stands the windmill, destroyed by fire in 1945.

MAIN STREET, WOODHOUSE had a roadside well with a fountain for public use. Water flowed from the bull's head for the refreshment of humans and horses. Its dedication in 1859 showed it to be a casting by William Taylor, bellfounder of Loughborough. The donor, Mrs Perry Herrick, was a strong supporter of the temperance movement so the village had no public house. She disliked idle gossip and Beaumanor estate cottages had their doors set so that it would be impossible to stand on the step and chat with a neighbour.

WHITWICK MARKET PLACE, as it was in the early twentieth century. It has its origins in the Middle Ages.

MAIN STREET, THORNTON in the 1920s had the calm air of a rural community.

CHARNWOOD HALL was given to Loughborough as a convalescent home by its first mayor, Joseph Griggs. In 1911 it still met the needs of those recovering from illnesses and operations. During the First World War wounded soldiers recuperated there. Several other benefactors gave similar convalescent homes in Charnwood, including Ellen Towle at Woodhouse Eaves. The hall has changed use several times, being at one time a residence for student teachers from Loughborough and now serving as a boarding house for pupils of Burleigh Community College, Loughborough.

THE SWANIMOTE OAK near Whitwick was an ancient landmark where the court of swineherds met annually from medieval times to share out the valuable rights to feed pigs in the forest. The whole area came under the jurisdictions of the lords of the manors of Shepshed, Whitwick and Groby.

THIS VIEW OF QUORN shows the River Soar in the top right and the main road that formed part of the principal route from Manchester to London. This road needed tolls for its upkeep during the eighteenth and first half of the nineteenth centuries. Inns in Quorn provided popular stopping places where horses could be changed and travellers refreshed. The canal enabled coal to be brought to the gasworks at the top right. Wright's mill, conspicuous by its tall chimney, manufactured elastic webbing for much of the British hosiery industry, and during the First World War supplied much of the webbing for the army. The situation of the village was partly determined by the flood plain of the river as well as by its crossroads position. It owed some of its prosperity to the services it supplied for the Quorn Hunt during the nineteenth century.

Halls and Houses

STEWARDS HAY AT GROBY was rebuilt in 1857 and renamed Bradgate House when the Seventh Earl of Stamford and Warrington became Master of the Quorn Hunt. It was demolished in 1926, with the exception of the stable block.

THE SUMMER HOUSE ON BARDON HILL was part of the Bardon Hall estate. It was erected during the eighteenth century and drawn by John Throsby in 1791. From this vantage point on a clear day visitors could enjoy views as far as Lincoln Cathedral, the Wrekin in Shropshire and Sugar Loaf mountain in South Wales, as well as the peaks of the Pennines in Derbyshire and even the uplands near Dunstable. This house was demolished after 1944.

THURCASTON PARISH CHURCH ROOF INTERIOR is a superb example of the timber construction methods used, not only in churches but also in the halls of large houses, during the Middle Ages and later. These beams supported heavy slates, tiles, lead sheeting or even extensive thatch.

A HUNTING BOX was a house used for shelter and as a base for hunters. This one was known as Gun Hill House near Whitwick and belonged to the De Lisles. Although now a ruin, it was occupied in its later days by a family.

SWITHLAND HALL was the home of the Danvers family, the Earls of Lanesborough, until the 1970s. Sir James Pennythorne designed a hall for the fourth Earl but it was destroyed by fire in 1822. The present hall was begun on a different site in 1834 and extended in 1852. The house has been divided into a number of private flats.

POTTER'S ROMANTIC VIEW OF CHARLEY HALL in 1842 makes the house on Charley Knoll look sylvan. It served as a residence for various gentlemen farmers and was the most prominent house in a dispersed hamlet.

CADEMAN'S HOUSE near the rocks of the same name on the Whitwick side of the Forest served the De Lisle family and guests as a hunting box in its heyday.

THE REAR ENTRANCE to the kitchen yard at Swithland Hall has an imposing design.

QUORN HALL, THE NETHER HALL, was built for Thomas Farnham around 1430, when he moved from the family seat. Extended in the seventeenth century, it was remodelled by Hugo Meynell to include an additional upper storey in 1790, and set in landscaped grounds. Edward Warner, hosiery manufacturer, reconstructed a new front in 1855. From 1928 until 1937 it served as a Country Club with twenty bedrooms and other facilities. Between 1938 and 1976 the Loughborough Colleges used it to accommodate fifty students. Today it houses foreign school parties on educational visits to Leicestershire.

QUORN HALL had a grand interior to match its external appearance.

LATIMERS HOUSE, THURCASTON.

ALLEGED TO BE THE BIRTH PLACE OF BISHOP HUGH LATIMER, this house was a fine example of cruck construction with a thatched roof. It was probably built in the fifteenth century and demolished early in the twentieth century.

GARENDON HALL was built in 1742 on the site of the Cistercian Abbey founded in 1133. The Palladian style was chosen by Ambrose Phillipps and his brother Samuel. Ambrose's daughter, Mary, married Edward de Lisle in the early eighteenth century.

AMBROSE MARCH PHILLIPPS DE LISLE commissioned E. W. Pugin to design a fourth storey for Garendon Hall in 1864. During the Second World War the army requisitioned the hall and the subsequent decay led to its demolition in 1964.

THE TRIUMPHAL ARCH IN GARENDON PARK was one of the follies erected in the eighteenth century in the classical style derived from Greco-Roman civilization. The park had a Temple of Venus and an Obelisk similar to Cleopatra's Needle. All three survive.

THE PONY AND CURRICLE accompanies some of the De Lisle family outside Garendon Hall around 1910.

THE BAVARIAN ARCH at Garendon Hall was designed by William Railton in 1834.

THE LODGE TO THE BEAUMANOR ESTATE had a more wooded aspect during the years between the world wars.

BEAUMANOR HALL was etched for Nichol's *History of Leicestershire* during the 1790s.

BEAUMANOR was finished in 1845 for William Perry Herrick, having been designed by William Railton, who also designed Nelson's Column. He chose the Jacobean style and the interior includes a dramatic grand staircase leading to the upper floor from the hall. The predecessor mansion was erected for Robert Herrick in 1725 following the design of John Westley. It stood on a different site and was demolished in 1841. The present house was financed from the profits of Herrick properties in Staffordshire as well as in Leicestershire. Coal contributed to much of the family fortune. William Perry Herrick and his sister were major benefactors of the Church of England in Leicestershire as well as other charities, including the building of the hospital in Loughborough.

VISCOUNT CURZON, heir to the Beaumanor estate, was married in 1907 at the parish church in Woodhouse Eaves.

MRS SOPHIA PERRY HERRICK in later life in a bathchair; she died in 1915 aged 83. She married her husband William when he was 66 and she was 34. She actively supported the Church of England by subscribing for the building of new parish churches in Leicester and the upkeep and extension of various others, including All Saints in Loughborough and the church at Copt Oak in the 1890s. She fostered teetotalism on the Beaumanor estate.

MRS PERRY HERRICK'S DONKEY-CARRIAGE enabled her to travel about the Beaumanor district, and it was also taken by rail for her use when she visited other family properties in Herefordshire and elsewhere.

THE LAKE OF GARRATS HEY AT WOODHOUSE provided facilities for skating in winter and fishing in season.

GARRATS HAY (once spelt Garrets Hey), Woodhouse, belonged to the Beaumanor estate until 1946, when it was sold to the War Office. It had been a farmhouse during the nineteenth century when members of the Herrick family lived there. At the beginning of the twentieth century it was the home of William Montague Curzon Herrick who died before succeeding to the estate. His widow married the Revd Faithfull, the local vicar, and the building was used as the vicarage for a time. In the Second World War the property formed part of a camp for the women of the Auxiliary Territorial Army (ATS). In the post-war years it became the officers' mess for the Royal Corps of Signals.

THE BRAND AT WOODHOUSE EAVES was built in 1870 and bought by the Martin family in 1887. The slate quarries in its grounds had ceased to be worked in the 1820s, and by the time of the house sale had become lakes known as Perch, Pike and Trout. The house was the home of Sir Robert Martin, who served as Chairman of Leicestershire County Council from 1924 until 1960. Concurrently he chaired the County Education Committee. Col. Sir Andrew Martin is the present owner.

THE SERVANTS POSE at the Brand, home of the Martin family, early in the twentieth century. There were six indoor and six outdoor servants. The butler stands in the back row, second from the left.

THE HOUSE ON THE GREEN at Anstey, owned by the Martin family, illustrates the visual attractions of timber-built housing that had the simultaneous virtues of allowing flexibility in alterations and good heat insulation.

THE SHIP AT ANSTEY belonged to the Martin family for generations. Its name derived from the very large number of timbers used in the construction of the house. Whether any ship's timbers were used is uncertain. Reputedly a calling house for monks travelling between Leicester Abbey and Ulverscroft Priory, the house was demolished in 1957.

THE DE LISLE FAMILY EMPLOYED GAMEKEEPERS whose housing, like this Keeper's Cottage, offered better accommodation than that enjoyed by the majority of people in the area. The high wages of these employees reflected both their responsibility for protecting their employers' property from poachers and the isolated social life that sometimes entailed threats to life and limb from some of the people caught poaching.

THE RANGER'S COTTAGE AT HUGGLESCOTE at the western edge of Charnwood Forest enabled the landowner to provide some continuous protection for game and timber. This cottage may have been erected in the eighteenth century, but disputes over rights to wild forest animals, brushwood and fruits had existed for many centuries.

DONINGTON-LE-HEATH MANOR HOUSE, now a museum, was reputed at the time of this photograph (early twentieth century) to be the oldest continuously inhabited building in Leicestershire. It was built in 1280 and had few subsequent alterations.

THE PEACEFUL SCENE of the early twentieth century in Newtown Linford contains brick, thatch, and timber constructions.

STONEYWELL COTTAGE AT MARKFIELD was built by Ernest Gimson in 1897/8. Gimson was born in Leicester in 1864 and studied architecture at the Leicester School of Art. His work as a furniture designer was influenced by William Morris and the campaign against fussy design and poor quality of domestic furniture. He learned the art of making rush-seated and wood-turned chairs and drew for inspiration on the craftsmen of the Middle Ages. The Gimson room in the Newark Houses Museum in Leicester displays the work. Stoneywell, Rockyfield and Lea cottages show his talents for blending buildings into the landscape and for using local materials.

BROOMBRIGGS HOUSE NEAR WOODHOUSE EAVES lies level with Beacon Hill. It was originally a cottage for a tenant farmer on the Beaumanor estate. Earlier in the twentieth century cattle were bred to stock farms in Argentina. At the time of the enclosures in the nineteenth century a Regency façade was added. The house and farm were sold in 1946 as part of the Beaumanor estate. In 1970 Mr and Mrs Charles Frears bought the property and gave the land to Leicestershire County Council to develop for public use. The Council laid out a farm trail for walkers and riders. This is a very exhilarating walk of around one and a half hours, up and down steep slopes, over stiles and past a variety of scenery. The house is now a private residence.

THE NEARER OF THESE NEWTOWN LINFORD COTTAGES in Post Office Row was of cruck design and was called Dingley Dell. This building method makes use of a large mature tree to provide the main structural timbers at either end of the house. These are tied at the roof ridge and at other key points by beams that support floors and walls. Walls were not necessarily load bearing and so the interior could be adapted to the needs of the inhabitants. The use of thatch was once common because it provided both a weatherproof roof and good thermal insulation. These dwellings became popular and new money arrived with the commuters who settled in growing numbers within Charnwood Forest villages during the twentieth century. Restoration in the 1960s and a garage at the end of the lane suggest affluence (below).

THIS TIMBER-FRAMED MANOR HOUSE AT THURCASTON was the seat of the Grosvenor family. It is now demolished.

MAIN STREET, MOUNTSORREL has a house of granite blocks constructed in 1707, and beyond it is a timber-framed house of 1617. The difference in building materials reflected availability and price.

A FAMILY stands next to Long Close House in Main Street, Woodhouse Eaves. Part of the house is reputed to have been built originally as a hunting lodge for King John.

FOWKE STREET IN ROTHLEY in the early twentieth century had houses of various dates and styles but all used local building materials.

HOLYWELL HAW (or Hall) was a cattle farm owned by Garendon Abbey. In 1535, the year before the abbey was dissolved, there was still pasture for twenty cattle. The word 'haw' means enclosure, usually by a thorn hedge; the term 'hall' may be a corruption of Haw. The 'holy well' is still to be found there, providing water of exceptional purity. There was a moated site at Holywell; it is possible that the house offered lodgings to people crossing in and out of Charnwood. The old house is adjacent to the new research centre of the Gas Council.

BLUEBELL COTTAGE AT NANPANTAN has a peaceful air. The windows had the sliding casements common in the East Midlands before the mid-nineteenth century.

KINCHLEY FARM is first recorded in 1656. The house was demolished in 1896 to make way for Swithland reservoir.

QUORN HOUSE was built by the Farnham family in 1820 after the Kaye House had been pulled down. The earliest building on this land had been the Over Hall. Quorn House stands in a large area of parkland. Nearby were stables and a watermill, neither of which remain. The house contained a billiard room, gun room, and carpentry room as well as reception and living rooms. Portraits of generations of Farnhams remind the family of their long history in the village.

SECTION FOUR

Making a Living

WHILE THE MILLER WORKS HARD to grind the grain, a group on an outing to Woodhouse Eaves enjoys the sights, sounds and smells of Windmill Hill.

SHEPSHED MARKET PLACE still fulfilled its original purpose during the early 1920s.

HULL AND SON, CATERERS AND BAKERS made deliveries from a horse-drawn van during the early years of the twentieth century.

OVER THE YEARS the flatter parts of the Charnwood heights have been cultivated, stones removed and fences and drystone walls built. The single horse drawing a plough in 1935 was working on a farm with Iveshead in the background. Tractors replaced horses on many farms during the years between 1939 and 1945.

THIS WELL-BUILT FARM in the Bowden Castle area of Charley parish has drystone walls enclosing its yard and gardens. These were made from the loose rocks that ploughing had revealed.

THE FARMER AND HIS FAMILY stand at White Leys farm, Jane Street, Coalville in 1894.

THE MATTS FAMILY farmed at Ulverscroft in the 1890s.

FORESTERS working near Grace Dieu, hauling timber for a sawmill. These scenes occurred in many parts of Charnwood Forest during both world wars when the difficulties of importation made the use of home grown wood a necessity. In the background is a viaduct of the Charnwood Forest Railway.

THE STEAM CRANE at Quorn and Woodhouse railway station sidings loading timber from the Beaumanor estate in 1926.

THE BRACKEN HARVEST at the Brand, Woodhouse Eaves in 1940 provided bedding for livestock in the winter. Sir Robert Martin, in the centre, supervises the work and John Atkin, the keeper, stands to the left by the horse's head. The horse was thirty-three years old. In earlier centuries burnt bracken was a source of lye for cleansing cloth.

THE CULTIVATION OF CHRISTMAS TREES by Pringle Forestry near Newtown Linford had reached an annual output of 10,000 trees in 1969. This form of farming began after 1926 when the government prohibited imports of foreign trees because of disease.

A DEMONSTRATION OF THE CRAFT OF THATCHING at Quorn in the mid-twentieth century.

STAFF AT THE HOTEL IN THRINGSTONE around 1900.

HOSIERY AND KNITWEAR were the dominant occupations in Shepshed during the eighteenth, nineteenth and early twentieth centuries. Hand-operated framework knitting machines were installed in cottages, usually on an upper floor with extra-large windows to make the most of the available light. In these cottages a doorway in the upper storey allowed the hoist to bring in machinery or to move goods in and out to waiting carts.

DOMESTIC PRODUCTION OF HOSE required seaming partly finished garments. The group of outworkers in Belton are handing over work.

THE LAST STOCKINGER IN SHEPSHED to have a framework knitting machine, Mr Needham, is shown using a winding wheel in the 1940s. He is 'back-winding', a process which recovers thread from a spoilt piece of hose.

AN ARTIST'S IMPRESSION from around 1840 shows the appearance of Mountsorrel with its principal features which included a windmill on the hill. This was demolished by the quarry company in the latter part of the nineteenth century.

ANSTEY MILL made use of the water power of Rothley Brook to drive a breast-shot wheel in 1872. This had a diameter of about 13 ft. The first mention of a mill on the site is in 1306 but its size is not known. Mills were profitable for landowners who usually required tenants to take their grain to the manorial mill. The mill shown is the result of extensive reconstruction in the early nineteenth century. The building ceased to be a mill in the early twentieth century.

THE WINDMILL AT WOODHOUSE EAVES was burned down in April 1945. Various proposals have been made to reconstruct it as a landmark. Windmill Hill was a very popular climb for the view from the summit.

FENNY SPRING MILL NEAR BLACKBROOK RESERVOIR ground grain in its heyday. The mill had become derelict by 1956 when it was bought and converted into a private house.

FENNY SPRING MILL was repaired and adapted as a private residence for Mr Bernard Fouquier in 1957. It had a brick-built tower capped by a revolving ogee housing for the two sails that powered the grinding stones. A small sail mechanism opposite the main sails kept the mill at work. Two sailed mills were unusual in Leicestershire.

THE GASWORKS AT SHEPSHED, shown here during the early twentieth century, had been in existence since the formation of the Sheepshead Gas Light Company in 1858.

THE BATES FAMILY were wheelwrights in Quorn throughout the nineteenth century. Joe Bates is transporting timber to his workshop.

EDWARD CARR was a boot and shoe repairer in Leicestershire Road, Quorn around 1930.

Religious Life

ST WINEFRIDE'S ROMAN CATHOLIC CHURCH, Pick Street, Shepshed.

MOUNT ST BERNARDS MONASTERY is set in its own farmland within Charnwood Forest. The donor of the land was the De Lisle family, converted to Roman Catholicism during the eighteenth century. They invited the Cistercian Order to supply the first regular religious house in the county and work began in the 1840s. The money for the first buildings came from the Earl of Shrewsbury. A.N.W. Pugin, the passionate Catholic advocate of the medieval style, was the architect.

THE DAILY ROUND in the abbey included prayers and religious devotions as well as mundane work on the abbey farm. Monks in their working habits are going to the fields in 1958. Since then tillage and many other tasks have been mechanized.

THE CALVARY at Mount St Bernards has always been accessible both to the community and to all lay visitors. Built on a natural outcrop of rock, the winding ascent gives a good view of the abbey buildings as well as serving spiritual and aesthetic purposes.

DAILY LIFE at Mount St Bernards Abbey in 1877 included feeding the pigs, discussion with the Abbot in the Chapter House, dining in the Refectory and reading in the Cloisters.

MONKS stacking clusters of sheaves into stooks (shocks) at harvest time in 1958 on the Mount St Bernards Abbey farm. This activity allowed drying to be completed before the crop went to the threshing floor. Mechanization with combine harvesters and driers has taken such hard manual work from almost all farms.

THE CALVARY AT THRINGSTONE was one of the demonstrations of faith by Roman Catholics who had become numerous by the end of the nineteenth century.

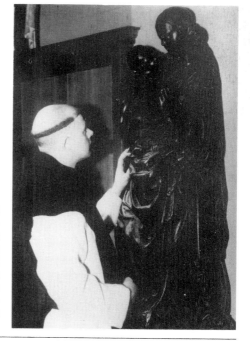

THE BLACK MADONNA, which originated at Hailes Abbey in Gloucestershire, was subsequently presented to Mount St Bernards Abbey and provides one of the links with pre-Reformation monasticism in England. It was carved at the beginning of the sixteenth century, removed from Hailes Abbey at the Dissolution and hidden during the persecution of Roman Catholics in the sixteenth and seventeenth centuries.

THE EARL OF LEICESTER founded Ulverscroft Priory before 1154, and the Augustinian Order was adopted. Although there were reports of bad management in 1438, Charley Priory was united with Ulverscroft in 1465 and a good report resulted. The house was in a wilderness area and refreshed many travellers. Nevertheless, it was closed in 1539. Some parts of the ruins still stand but are not open to the public.

ROLEIA (Rothley) was king's land in 1086. The Order of the Knights Templar was begun in 1118 by nine French knights to protect pilgrims against the infidels on the way to the holy city of Jerusalem. Each knight wore a white mantle with a red cross and took a vow of poverty that often resulted in there being only one horse for two men. In 1140 they came to England and were later given the chapel in Rothley manor. Sir John de Harcourt was given the manor for services to King John and he died subsequently fighting the Saracens. Pope Clement V dissolved the Templars in 1312 and their assets in England were passed to the Knights of St John of Jerusalem. This order lost its assets in 1536 during the Reformation. Humphrey Babington bought the manor in 1544 and used the house as a private residence. One of his descendants, Thomas Babington Macaulay (later Lord) wrote the *History of England* as well as campaigning for the abolition of slavery in the British Empire. In the 1960s the manor house was converted into a hotel and restaurant.

ROTHLEY TEMPLE CHAPEL INTERIOR in 1914 with the walls adorned by hatchments, the funerary memorials of former owners of Rothley Court. At one time the banners of the knights brought colour to the building.

LOUGHBOROUGH AND DISTRICT ARCHAEOLOGICAL SOCIETY in 1965 began to excavate the site of the Cistercian Abbey of Garendon, which had been founded in 1133 by the Earl of Leicester. The original land had been so poor that it was a challenge to the Cistercians to improve it. So successful had the abbey been that by the time of the Dissolution of the Monasteries it owned over 1,000 acres of farmland in Leicestershire. It had also acquired a coal mine, three stone quarries, four watermills, sheep walks, fishing rights and property in many towns. The first monks wore white habits of undyed wool, had a vegetarian diet taken in one daily meal, rejected luxury to sleep on straw, and renounced personal wealth. Their time was spent in private devotion and manual labour. The abbey was destroyed almost completely in 1536 and Garendon Hall was later built on the site.

THE COFFIN LID indicates that the deceased was probably one of the Abbots of Garendon.

THE STONE COFFIN associated with the lid contained an abbot's remains.

THE CHAPTER HOUSE was the room set aside for decision making. The pillars supported the roof.

THE MAIN DRAIN of Garendon Abbey was constructed in the thirteenth century and it removed sewage and kitchen waste. A large pool in the grounds supplied water for flushing. The blocks of dressed sandstone came from elsewhere in the country.

GRACE DIEU MANOR stands in the grounds of the former Augustinian Priory. It was built for Ambrose Lisle March Phillipps de Lisle to designs by William Railton in 1833/34. A.N.W. Pugin oversaw some of the alterations at the manor and his ideas found expression in the chapel. The house served for a time as a church for local Catholics. The De Lisles leased the house to various tenants of whom Charles Booth was the most celebrated in the latter part of the nineteenth century. The manor now houses a Roman Catholic Preparatory School for boys and girls.

GRACE DIEU PRIORY was founded for nuns known as Augustinian Canonesses between 1235 and 1240. They lived wholly within the priory. In 1535 a commission of local gentry found that the nuns were virtuous, but against their wishes the house was closed in 1538. The property was then bought by the Beaumonts, the most famous of whom was Francis Beaumont who, with John Fletcher, wrote successful plays during the early seventeenth century including *The Knight of the Burning Pestle*. The residential part of the priory was pulled down by Ambrose Phillipps in 1696.

THE ROMAN CATHOLIC CHURCH OF THE HOLY CROSS at Whitwick as it was soon after completion in 1904.

CHARLES BOOTH AND HIS FAMILY pictured at Grace Dieu Manor in 1914. His family had made its fortune as shipowners in Liverpool, where he became deeply interested in the social problems of poverty. He undertook the first large scale quantitative study of poverty and deprivation in London. He became the president of the Royal Statistical Society and was a member of the Royal Commission on the Poor Law appointed at the beginning of the twentieth century. He was a prominent advocate of old age pensions which were introduced in 1908.

CHRIST CHURCH PARSONAGE AND SCHOOL at Coalville were dedicated in 1838 when the development of the coalfield had made Long Lane a community of sufficient size to need a separate parish. The buildings had been finished in 1836 but lack of funds delayed their use.

ST MARY'S PARISH CHURCH AT ROTHLEY stands on the site where a church is believed to have existed in the eleventh century. The building contains a Norman font dating from 1160 and some Babington family monuments from the seventeenth century. The church was much altered when the chancel was rebuilt in 1877. The churchyard has many slate gravestones.

ST JOHN THE BAPTIST CHURCH OF ENGLAND AT WHITWICK underwent extensive restoration work in the mid-nineteenth century and again in the 1890s. It was the only parish church on the western side of the forest until the rapid population increases in the early part of the nineteenth century led to the formation of new parishes.

A.N.W. PUGIN DESIGNED THIS CHURCH in Pick Street, Shepshed for the Roman Catholic parish of St Winefride. Consecrated in 1842, it ceased to serve as a church in 1968. The missionary work of Father Gentili of the Rosminian Order had notable success among some of the impoverished framework knitters, whose livelihoods had been undermined by developments in machine-made hosiery and textiles during the 1820s. Gentili stressed that poverty had no place in Christian teaching and that faith ought to provide solace in times of distress. Associated with the church was a presbytery and a school, both now demolished. The former church is now a private house.

THE FEAST OF CORPUS CHRISTI is held on the Thursday following Trinity Sunday. The commemoration of the sacrament of the body of Christ by the faithful took place in the late spring. This Roman Catholic procession of celebration was at Shepshed around 1914.

WOODHOUSE EAVES became the ecclesiastical parish of St Paul in 1837, when the church of England reorganized its ministry. The ancient parish of Barrow-upon-Soar was divided into four parts: Barrow, Quorn, Woodhouse and Woodhouse Eaves.

THE MEDIEVAL MARKET CROSS OF MOUNTSORREL was made around 1500 and once stood in Baron Lane. It was removed to Swithland Hall in 1793 by Sir John Danvers to adorn the park and in exchange he had the Buttermarket built in Mountsorrel. Market crosses were often used to decorate a vista in a park.

A NINTH-CENTURY SAXON CROSS in the churchyard of Rothley parish church once served as the meeting place for the priests who came from mission centres (minsters) to preach the gospel to local people. It was sited so that the priest stood above the congregation.

THE DEDICATION of the parish church of Shepshed is to St Botolph, patron of travellers. The church was built in the eleventh century. A pancake bell was rung on Shrove Tuesdays and a curfew at eight each evening. By the early twentieth century the building had some unusual features, including a broach-spire that climbs in two separate gradients.

AS LOCAL SQUIRES of Shepshed, the Phillipps family occupied a special pew in St Botolph's and many of their names are recorded on memorial tablets.

THE MEMORIAL TO THE GREY FAMILY in the chapel of Bradgate House in Bradgate Park commemorates one of the major families of the nobility during the first half of the sixteenth century. The most celebrated member was Lady Jane.

THE SHEEP'S HEAD OF SHEPSHED adorns St Botolph's parish church. The parish name was spelt Sheepshead until the 1890s, when a phonetic rendering was adopted for official documents.

THE FARNHAM FAMILY have lived in Quorn since the thirteenth century at the Over Hall, later rebuilt as Quorn House, and at the Nether Hall later called Quorn Hall. The Farnham chapel in St Bartholomew's church contains several important memorials including those of John Farnham and his wife, Dorothy.

THE SLAB IN THURCASTON CHURCH records the birth in 1475 of Hugh Latimer, who became a Bishop of Worcester. He was burnt as an incorrigible heretic at Oxford in 1555 during the reign of the Roman Catholic Queen Mary. He is now commemorated as one of the Protestant martyrs.

ST MARY IN CHARNWOOD is a small church just above Nanpantan crossroads and a daughter church of Emmanuel parish in Loughborough. It was built in 1888 on land later donated by E.W. Warner of Nanpantan Hall in 1896 and provided the only place of worship for the hamlet of Nanpantan. A new vestry was added in 1960.

FIELD STREET METHODIST CHURCH IN SHEPSHED was built in 1878 in a style that reflected the Wesleyan tradition. The building included not only the place of worship but rooms for Sunday school, Bible study and other meetings. It offered a whole way of life. The church was refurbished in the late 1960s so that it could house all Methodists, and was renamed Christ Church.

BELTON GENERAL BAPTIST CHURCH was erected in 1813 to serve the village and surrounding district. The entrance for the meetings of deacons and the Sunday school was by the small door at the side of the building. The simplicity and homeliness of the building contrasts with the formal decorated architecture of parish churches. At the rear is the graveyard that came into use after the 1853 Burial Act.

THE BISHOP OF LINCOLN dedicated the chapel at the Oaks on 18 June 1815, the day of the Battle of Waterloo. The area lay within the 'peculiar' of Groby; this meant it was outside the parish network that covered most of England. To pay for the clergyman, land was assigned from the area enclosed by the Charnwood Enclosure Act of 1808. The building costs were met by subscriptions raised from landowners within the Charnwood Forest area.

A CHRISTENING at St Bartholomew's church, Quorn at the beginning of the twentieth century.

THE WESLEYAN METHODISTS wanted their own church in Quorn and the foundation stone was laid at a ceremony held on 1 April 1907. It opened in September the same year having cost £1,714.

SECTION SIX
Getting About

THE ISLAND PLATFORM of Rothley station (typical of the Great Central Railway) opened in 1898, just before this picture was taken.

THE LEICESTERSHIRE YEOMANRY at Woodhouse during May 1911 were on a training exercise. At this time many military commanders believed cavalry had a major role to play in modern warfare. This regiment had served in the Boer War of South Africa a decade earlier.

COALVILLE CO-OPERATIVE SOCIETY'S HORSES are being prepared for military service on 11 August 1914. War had been declared on 4 August and in the euphoria it was expected that the war would be over by Christmas. Horse-drawn ambulances were sent from the local mines to the front at the same time.

THE JACQUES FAMILY OF MOUNTSORREL in 1905 ride in a Stanhope Phaeton (perhaps a New Zephyr made by John Warren of Loughborough), a vehicle developed for town and country use.

THE HORSE still had the monopoly on short distance transport in Coalville High Street before 1914, but the car in the shadows is an omen for the future.

A BOY ENJOYS PADDLING in the ford near Ulverscroft during the 1930s. The level of water varied according to the depth of the stream that was often in flood. Most fords have since been bridged and culverted.

THE LOCK-KEEPER works the lock next to his cottage by the canal at Mountsorrel. The narrowboats were used to carry coal to such villages as Quorn and take loads of Mountsorrel granite to London and elsewhere.

THE ARCHED PACKHORSE BRIDGE AT ANSTEY was still in use at the beginning of the twentieth century. The lower picture shows the refuges where people could stand aside to allow laden packhorses to pass. Many of these bridges proved unsuitable for modern traffic.

LATIMER'S BRIDGE AT THURCASTON had little traffic passing over it in 1922.

THIS SECTION OF THE CHARNWOOD FOREST CANAL near Shepshed formed part of a canal built in the mid-1790s to bring coal from west Leicestershire near Thringstone to Loughborough. The canal terminated at Nanpantan and a narrow gauge railway was built to carry the coal down to Loughborough for onward carriage by the canalized River Soar. The canal failed in 1799 (see p. 120).

THE CHARNWOOD FOREST CANAL passed through this brick-lined tunnel near Shepshed. The canal was built to follow as closely as possible the 300 ft contour line so as to avoid the cost of making locks and incurring the expense of additional reservoir capacity. This tunnel shows the tow-paths laid on either side for the horses pulling the barges.

THESE NAVVIES were working on Woodthorpe Cutting, part of the Great Central Railway, in the mid-1890s. The arrival of the navvies sometimes worried local people because of their rough manners and rowdy behaviour. To combat these problems the churches set up mission huts served by special clergy. High wages were earned by the navvies in some of the most physically demanding and dangerous conditions. By the mid-1890s contractors used steam-driven excavators for some digging, but there still remained much manual labour.

THE SWANNINGTON INCLINE, near Coalville, had a gradient of 1 in 17 over its length of about 670 metres. It had a stationary steam engine at its head to haul the loaded wagons of coal up the slope by cable. The incline opened in 1843 to raise coal from the Swannington area up to Coalville, from where it went by normal railway to Leicester or other destinations. Whenever the engine failed horses were used. All the wagons were fitted with double brakes. The use of the incline was never great and diminished after 1870 because the location of coal production moved away from Swannington.

THE LONDON & NORTH WESTERN RAILWAY STEAM RAILCAR stands at the Whitwick station platform at the beginning of the twentieth century. These vehicles were used regularly between the Loughborough terminus of the Charnwood Forest Railway and the main line junction at Nuneaton. They had an inadequately lagged boiler that made the passenger compartment uncomfortably warm.

RAILWAY ENTHUSIASTS AT SHEPSHED are showing interest in the final, specially chartered, passenger train to run on the Charnwood Forest Railway on 8 September 1962. Freight trains ran from Loughborough to Coalville and Nuneaton until 11 December 1963. The railway had opened on 11 April 1883.

A STEAM LOCOMOTIVE crosses the main thoroughfare in the centre of Coalville.

ONE OF THE EARLIEST PRIVATE CARS in Belvoir Road, Coalville, around the time of the First World War, encouraging pedestrians to keep to the pavement. The new Lloyds Bank building and the Coalville electric cinema herald the modern age.

A TRIUMPH CHARABANC takes an outing of the employees of White and Smith of Shepshed in the early 1920s.

SECTION SEVEN

Reservoirs

THORNTON RESERVOIR was constructed in Charnwood Forest in 1853 by Leicester Corporation to supply its rapidly growing population. These waters are used for fishing and sailing and widen the scope of leisure activities.

CROPSTON RESERVOIR lies next to Bradgate Park and is shown here after completion of the dam in 1866. Patches of water are gathering at the bottom of the valley.

CROPSTON RESERVOIR was photographed two years later in 1868 when the initial flooding of the valley was nearing completion. This water was to benefit the industrial and domestic users in Leicester. Not only was the town's population rapidly growing, but many homes were being connected to a piped water supply for the first time. The following years were to prove that an increase in life expectation owed much to clean water and a new sewage system.

ARCHDEACON FEARON OF LOUGHBOROUGH persuaded some businessmen to draft a parliamentary bill to establish a water company in 1866. Nanpantan reservoir provided Loughborough with its first piped water supply in 1870. Before that time the only water available was from wells and streams. The high death rate from cholera and typhoid was reduced by an adequate sewage system and clean water. After 1870 life expectancy increased, and industries dependent on steam power or which used water for cleaning and dyeing benefited greatly.

SWITHLAND RESERVOIR was constructed in the 1890s to meet the rapidly growing demands for water from Leicestershire. The picture shows the slow sand filter plant, dam and overflow channel for the River Lin (Buddon Brook) in 1940. Most of the wood has since been felled and the new quarry has approached to within 50 metres of the reservoir.

THE FULL EXTENT OF THE VIADUCT, built for the Great Central Railway, was exposed when Swithland reservoir was drained in 1976. This picture shows one of the last British Rail trains to cross.

JOHN POTTER, the Loughborough artist, at work by the River Lin, probably in the early 1890s. When Swithland reservoir was drained in 1976 remnants of the small bridge were revealed.

BLACKBROOK RESERVOIR EARTH DAM was begun in 1792 to provide water for the Charnwood Forest Canal (see pp. 108 and 109). The breach was made when quickly thawing snow in 1799 caused its collapse, and a torrent of water swept down to the River Soar, causing much damage in its path through the edge of Loughborough. The compensation costs prevented repairs and the Charnwood Forest Canal no longer functioned. The picture dates from a few years before the construction of the present reservoir.

BLACKBROOK RESERVOIR DAM was in the course of construction around 1904. It contained waters from the Blackbrook that rises in Charnwood Forest. Its purpose was to meet the increasing needs of Leicestershire, Loughborough and Shepshed. For example, Loughborough's population had grown from just over 11,000 in 1871 to 21,000 in 1901.

BLACKBROOK RESERVOIR DAM approached completion for its subsequent opening in 1906. The depth of water next to the dam is 68 ft and the length of the dam is 482 ft. An inspection tunnel the length of the dam, involving many steps up and down, has provided an extra excitement for visiting school parties over the years. On 11 February 1957 an earth tremor caused 12 ft coping stones to be removed from their settings and some temporary cracks appeared in the dam allowing much water to escape.

THE FOREST RESERVOIR ENVIRONMENTS provide quiet secluded habitats for birds. Many are water birds; some visitors, some resident. They live by streams, reservoirs, springs, plantations and parkland. Some of the most common are heron, mallard, teal, duck, pheasant, moorhen, coot, snipe, woodcock, pigeon, woodpecker, tit, wren, thrush, robin, willow-warbler, wagtail, sparrow, bullfinch, chaffinch, cormorant, mute swan and kingfisher. The little ringed plover is a wading bird and nests on stones in the open around the water margins. It is still listed as an endangered species and therefore is a success story in our area.

THE SPARROWHAWK nearly became extinct in the 1960s because of chemical pesticides that are now banned. They nest up in the trees and are predators who bring other dead birds to feed their young. The quiet areas of the reservoirs have attracted them.

SECTION EIGHT

Mines and Quarries

A BLOCKER cutting setts by hand at Mountsorrel quarry. These setts were used for paving roads and especially pavement edges.

A VERY EARLY SCENE at Broad Hill quarry at Mountsorrel. Mr Jackson started working Mountsorrel Hill in 1812 and soon employed 100 men. Later, William Martin took over and had doubled the workforce by 1850. In 1868 granite cost 5s. a ton. It was so hard that large pieces could only be broken by a 30 lb sledge hammer. Before tarmac was invented roads were roughly covered by loose broken granite. By 1929 two inch pieces of granite mixed with hot tar were finished off with a coat of half inch chippings. The row of covered huts to the left housed the men who chipped away to make setts.

A STEAM LOCOMOTIVE hauls a train of wagons with stone from the Mountsorrel quarry to connect with the main line.

THE LARGEST SINGLE-SPAN BRICK ARCH BRIDGE IN ENGLAND was erected in 1867 over the River Soar, to carry Mountsorrel granite by mineral railway either to the Midland Railway main line near Sileby or to the wharf for loading into waiting barges on the canalized Soar. The Grand Union Canal had been used before the railway to take stone by barge to places as far away as London.

THIS SCENE AT MOUNTSORREL QUARRY shows considerable progress, with steam lorries and steam loaders increasing the speed of production.

THIS AERIAL VIEW OF BROAD HILL QUARRY, MOUNTSORREL shows workings in the 1930s. The crushing and loading plants are right of centre and the railway lines go to the canal bank and towards the main line (bottom right). The long narrow village trapped between the hilly area and the flood plain of the Soar can be clearly seen. The stretch of water is the canal.

THE MOUNTSORREL QUARRY OPERATION was extended to Buddon Wood in 1906 and Cocklow quarry was opened. A mineral line enabled quick removal of granite. During the Second World War it was closed, and used as a firing range by American troops. In 1966 the Redland Roadstone group reopened it and extended the Buddon Wood operation in the 1970s.

MARKFIELD OLD QUARRY in the 1870s had a stream-driven crushing plant to make roadstone. The railway wagons in the foreground are taking the prepared stone by a mineral line that joined the Leicester and Swannington Line north of Battle Flat.

THIS OLD SLATE QUARRY is sited in Swithland Woods. The purple-green rock had been quarried since Roman times. The rock splits easily and could be made into slabs of various thicknesses. In the late eighteenth century it was transported to London by canal. Since closure the quarries have collected water to a great depth.

THIS HORSE-GIN was a hoist used in Swithland quarries from the eighteenth century to raise large baskets of slate from the quarry bottom. Horses walked away from the edge and pulled a rope attached to the wheel. Steam engines replaced horses during the nineteenth century. After 1860 there was much competition from Welsh slate quarries. These were served by railways and delivered cheaper slate. For this reason all Swithland quarries closed in 1887.

CHARNWOOD GRAVEYARDS contain many tombstones made from Swithland slate. Other slate products were roofing tiles, cheese presses, cattle troughs, floor tiles, walling, milestones, clockfaces and steps.

THE ARC (AMEY ROADSTONE COMPANY) CHARNWOOD QUARRY at Shepshed was being worked during the Victorian period and provided employment for people in the Shepshed area. The old Newhurst quarry scene shows working down to two levels, and in 1991 it has reached five levels. Plans have been made to increase the depth of the workings for years to come. The Longcliffe quarry joined to this one is nearly exhausted. In earliest days stone was moved by horse and cart and later by rail to join the Charnwood Forest Railway. This ceased in 1962 and now all goes by road. In 1960 65 men quarried around 800 tons a day. Demands for motorway construction from the 1960s necessitated the installation of much new machinery. Very soon fewer men quarried 4,000 tons a day.

THE STONE BLASTED FROM THE QUARRY FACE was originally moved by horse and cart. Later, 15 ton dumper lorries carried it up to the crushers. Since 1979 huge conveyor belts have replaced the lorries.

THE CART CARRYING GRANITE ROAD STONE in 1895 has just passed the weighbridge house of the bottom quarry at Forest Rock, Coalville.

THIS VIEW OF WHITWICK COLLIERY in 1956 shows the winding gear of one of the eight shafts then working. The pits were closed in 1986 and much of this area of the Leicestershire coalfield is now worked out of deep mined coal.

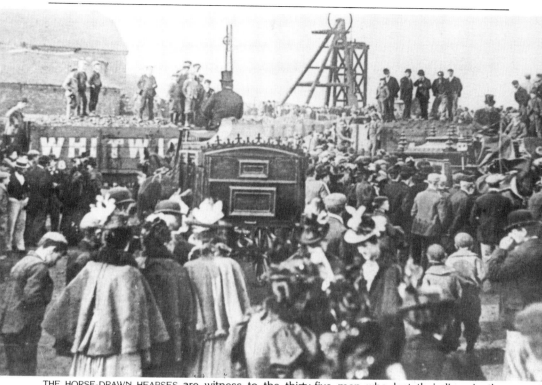

THE HORSE-DRAWN HEARSES are witness to the thirty-five men who lost their lives in the Whitwick colliery disaster, the single most serious accident in the West Leicestershire coalfield. Families and mourners waited anxiously for news for many hours but a few bodies had to remain underground. The cause of the disaster was a 'gob' fire.

THRINGSTONE MINE tapped coal measures laid down 250 million years ago. The simple design of headstock was common in the mid-nineteenth century when the development of the West Leicestershire coalfield began to gather momentum.

THE STEAM-DRIVEN COLLIERY PUMP AT WHITWICK was erected in 1827 and dismantled a century later. The long life of the pump can be attributed partly to the reliability of the crude but simple mechanism and partly to the cheapness of the fuel used to heat the boilers.

Enjoyment

THE MOUNTSORREL MAYPOLE in the early twentieth century gave much pleasure each year to the younger generations.

LOUGHBOROUGH CHORAL SOCIETY on their outing to the Pocket Gate rocks in 1911. The forest area was for years a popular destination for annual outings and treats. At this time many parties walked to their venue or took horse-drawn wagonettes.

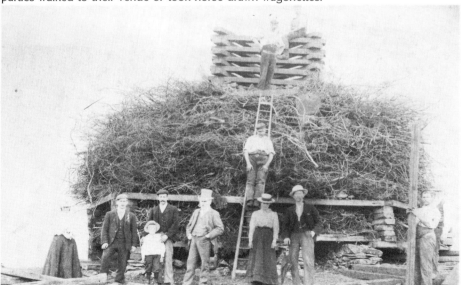

THE TOP OF THE BEACON HILL has always been a place where bonfires could be seen for miles around. This bonfire was built to celebrate the coronation of King Edward VII and Queen Alexandra in 1902. It stood 40 ft high and flames shot another 60 ft above that. It consumed 30 tons of firewood, 40 tons of brushwood, 26 tons of coal and 250 gallons of oil.

A HUGE BONFIRE was constructed near Whitwick to celebrate the coronation of King George V in 1911.

SIMPLE PLEASURES AND PASTIMES of the 1930s are reflected in this scene from Swithland Woods.

IN SOME YEARS the ice froze sufficiently to allow folk of all ages to gather for skating. February 1895 was such a time at Groby pool.

STUDENTS MAKING THEIR FINAL PREPARATIONS at Loughborough College in 1921 before competing in the Beacon Hill Race by car and motor cycle. Similar events had been organized before the First World War by keen motorists.

CELEBRATIONS to mark the coronation of King George V and Queen Mary outside the Crown and Cushion at Whitwick.

HUGO MEYNELL, 'the father of English fox-hunting', was master of the Quorn Hunt from 1753 until 1800 and lived at Quorn Hall. At that time Charnwood Forest was far more open and was a good school for young hounds. In Meynell's time the enclosure of the land meant that horses had to be taught to jump hedges and fences. Quorn Hall and other large houses in Quorn made the village a centre for large hunting parties as the sport grew in popularity.

TOM FIRR, the huntsman of the Quorn, is seen here on Whitelegs performing an impossible anatomical feat as he is depicted by the artist. Firr led the Quorn field for twenty-six seasons. After an accident in 1899 he gave up hunting.

THIS FARRIER worked with stage-coach horses and later settled in his smithy at the rear of the White Horse in Quorn. He was one of many farriers attending to the needs of the hunt in the 1890s. All forms of horse-drawn transport needed his skills.

THERE WERE THREE BLACKSMITHS SHOPS in Quorn in the mid-nineteenth century and many others in the Charnwood Forest area. This one was opposite The Blacksmiths public house in Meeting Street. Over 100 horses were shod here each summer in readiness for the hunting season. The smith made and repaired farm implements and also made garden railings. This building is now a private home.

THE QUORN HUNT PONY CLUB met at the Brand in 1990, keeping alive the social and geographical connection with Charnwood. The huntsman, Michael Farrins, is on the right.

THESE FOLK IN SHEPSHED are displaying some of the animals and equipment they used for their shooting parties around 1900. Guns, gundogs, ferreting dogs and what appears to be a monkey are shown alongside a gamebird.

THE QUORN HUNT met at Garendon Hall before the First World War when Charnwood formed Tuesday Country for the hunt.

THE BADGER is one of the most common mammals in Charnwood. The light sandy soils with coppices and woodland provide an ideal habitat for this nocturnal creature.

THE FOX is a common mammal that has been hunted for centuries. It relies for food on rabbits and other small animals. Many people report sightings of foxes crossing roads and appearing near towns and villages. It is far more urbanized than of old.

SIR ROBERT MARTIN demonstrating to a group of boys the way to sharpen an axe at a camp in Charnwood during the 1930s.

THIS OUTING TO THE HANGINGSTONE ROCK in Charnwood was the venue in August 1898 for the Leicester Volunteers and their friends and families. The Volunteers were the predecessors of the present day Territorial Army. The party travelled from Quorn and Woodhouse station by wagonette in the morning and were then collected in the evening.

SCOUTS pose with their master, the Revd Walters, outside his vicarage at Whitwick on 16 May 1914. Prior to his induction to the living at Whitwick, Mr Walters had been on the Dorset coast, in an area that included Brownsea Island, and he had acted as chaplain to Baden-Powell and the first scout camps. The scouting movement in Whitwick was started by Mr Walters, whose son, Mervyn, became a prominent figure in the movement for many years in Leicestershire, especially in the Loughborough district.

SHEPSHED ADULT SCHOOL ORCHESTRA, in 1916, reflected the strength of the creative use of leisure that characterized the Adult Schools movement. This movement began in the early nineteenth century and had strong support from evangelicals within the Church of England and from many Nonconformist churches. It had the ultimate purpose of increasing people's awareness of others. Associated with these influences were the self-improvement and self-advancement that education was expected to provide.

THE SUNDAY SCHOOL of the Baptist church in Charnwood Road, Shepshed had a day out to see the recently completed reservoir at Blackbrook. This provided a conveniently local venue that would combine education with entertainment and fresh air.

A FANCY DRESS PARADE in Mountsorrel in the summer of 1914. The cyclist carries a banner concerning fund-raising for the Leicester Royal Infirmary. This hospital was heavily dependent on charitable efforts and many public fund-raising events were needed to collect money.

THE PEOPLE OF BELTON prepare for a Mayday celebration before the First World War. Mayday at this time was an informal holiday. Most celebrations were focussed on village life.

THE FAIR AT BELTON in the final stages of preparation in 1909. Fairs at that time had become events devoted to pleasure rather than to trade. The presence of the policeman may have been in anticipation of trouble on account of longstanding rivalries between neighbouring villages.

THIS DEER among the bracken in Bradgate Park in 1948 symbolizes the original purpose of the park as a hunting ground. Another species, the Muntjack (not shown), has been introduced from Asia in recent years. It is a shy, nocturnal creature the size of a large dog and has now spread to many parts of Charnwood, where it lives unaided by man.

CHARLES BENNION, managing director of the British United Shoe Company, bought Bradgate Park in 1928 and presented it to the City of Leicester and the County. The park was 828 acres with a stone wall around it four and a half miles long. Bennion's wish was that wildlife should be preserved and that the public should have access. In 1976 the visitor centre at Marion's Cottage was opened to give information and sell gifts.

OLD JOHN TOWER was built as a folly by the fifth Earl of Stamford in 1786. There had, according to Nichols, been a windmill on the site in 1745. It has variously been a meeting place, a lookout tower, a vantage point and a high point on which to celebrate by lighting a bonfire, such as at the coming of age of the sixth Earl of Stamford.

THE OFFICIAL OPENING CEREMONY to make a present of Bradgate Park was held in 1928. Since then it has been a source of pleasure to the urban and rural population of the surrounding district. So many people walk there that a real danger of footpath erosion exists. The park staff are headed by the ranger and head-keeper. Part of their job is to make sure the numbers of deer are correct, to fell and plant trees and, more recently, to attempt to reintroduce some heather. There is a great variety of birds, mammals, reptiles, amphibians and fish to protect and encourage.

BRADGATE is not good farmland mainly because of the hard rocks beneath and the poor quality of the soil above. It has been a deer park since the twelfth century. There have been up to 130 red and 170 fallow deer. Sometimes cast-off antlers are mounted and sold. In earlier centuries antlers yielded translucent membranes to shield outdoor lamps ('lantern' derives from 'lamphorn'). In severe weather extra fodder is supplied for the deer. Other animals within the park have included horses, cattle, sheep and rabbits. The latter were introduced as a food source. J. Martin sketched the deer in Charnwood early in Victoria's reign.

THIS SUBSTANTIAL WATERFALL on the River Lin is one of five along its course. Their purpose is to aerate the waters before they enter Cropston reservoir. This area of Bradgate was long ago called Little Matlock because of its more rugged appearance. Also illustrated are the trees, grass and bracken which comprise the park's natural vegetation.

THE RIVER LIN is near to the Newtown Linford entrance to Bradgate Park. The complete course of this stream is unique in that it has its source in the hills, enters both Cropston and Swithland reservoirs in turn and then moves down to join the River Soar in the valley. Thus it reflects many varied wildlife habitats along its course. For part of its journey it is often known as Buddon Brook.

THE UNITED STATES 82ND AIRBORNE DIVISION was stationed in various locations within the Charnwood Forest in the months before their invasion drop into Normandy on D-day, 6 June 1944. Sir Robert Martin, Cyril Osborne (later knighted and MP for Louth) and Lady Hazelrigg met some of the American troops in Bradgate Park.

BRADGATE RUINS have lent themselves as a background to pageants and many other recreational activities throughout the twentieth century.

THOMAS GREY succeeded to the manor of Groby in 1501 and his family moved to the recently built mansion in Bradgate Park. This unfortified country house was made of locally fired bricks. The Great Hall had the family living quarters in the east end and servants' quarters in the west end. In 1530, Henry Grey, later Duke of Suffolk, succeeded to the property. His daughter, Lady Jane, was proclaimed queen in 1553 and reigned for nine days. Mary Tudor became queen and in 1554 Lady Jane was beheaded. After 1719 the old house started to decay and was ruinous by 1789.

ROTARIANS, whose charitable works included securing Swithland Wood for the people of Leicestershire, met at Bradgate Park in the 1930s. The trustees of the park also care for Swithland Wood.

WITHIN SWITHLAND WOODS are the remains of several derelict slate quarries that have become havens for varieties of wildlife. This beautiful wood comprises deciduous trees, mainly mature oaks. Leicester Rotary Club gave these woods to the public in 1931.

THE BLUEBELLS in woodland near Woodhouse Eaves have been a major spring attraction for many years to many people from nearby towns. Their presence indicates that the woods have long been kept in their natural state.

THE INAUGURATION OF THE TOPOSCOPE ON BEACON HILL enabled visitors to this popular landmark to identify the sights in all directions from the eastern highpoint of Charnwood Forest. Sir Robert Martin, to the right of the picture, represented Leicestershire County Council at the ceremony.

CHARNWOOD FOREST GOLF CLUB was founded in 1890 and is the oldest in Leicestershire. Mrs Perry Herrick allowed part of the Beaumanor estate around Hangingstone Rocks to be used as a nine-hole golf course. In 1915 the new owner, the Hon. William Montague Curzon Herrick, charged a £25 rent and allowed Sunday play. Caddies fees were 8 d. for nine holes. In 1946 the club bought the course of 77 acres for £2,570 in the sale of the Beaumanor estate. The natural features – slopes, rocks, trees, rhododendrons and bracken – make the course very attractive as well as providing natural hazards. The other forest courses, at Longcliffe (1909), Rothley Park (1915) and Lingdale (1967), have been made accessible by modern forms of transport. The picture shows a rocky outcrop in the 1950s which is now hidden by trees and bushes.

PERHAPS THE OLDEST FORM OF LEISURE in the forest is rambling, whether as part of an organized club or as an individual's urge to get up and go. There can be no better way to learn about and enjoy the forest area. Here the Loughborough and District CHA Rambling Club appear at the Cropston entrance to Bradgate Park. We hope that many more town and country dwellers will decide to get up and go and see their wonderful heritage.

ACKNOWLEDGEMENTS

Our grateful thanks are due to many people and organizations who have given us information and permission to use their photographs and other illustrations. We have sought to trace copyright owners but any who have been omitted should let us know so that we can include them in listings for any new edition of this book.

For photographs and illustrations we thank:
Leicestershire Museums and Library Service at the County Record Office; Central Library, Granby Street, Loughborough; Public Library, Hall Croft, Shepshed; Public Library, Coalville; and the following people, organizations and companies: Amey Roadstone Company, Dennis Baker and 150 Group of Coalville, John Bowen-Jones, British Coal, P. John Cox, G. Duffin, Grace Dieu Preparatory School, George Farnham, Colin Green, Peter W. Jones ARPS, Vera Kirk, *The Leicester Topic, The Limit* (Loughborough College Magazine), Col. Sir Andrew and Lady Martin, The Abbot and Community of Mount St Bernards Abbey, Redland Aggregates plc, Rothley Court Hotel management, G. Smith, T. Mervyn Ll. Walters, Noel Wakeling, Whitwick Historical Society, Brian C.J. Williams.

For information and help we thank:
Brian Antrobus, Dennis Baker, G.H. Barker, Mr and Mrs M. Bertioli, Eric Briers, G. Allen Chinnery, Revd Fr Duffy, Eric Davies, G. Eason, Colin Green, Robin Jenkins, Brother Jonathan, Stephen Kettle, D.J. Knighton, Col. Sir Andrew and Lady Martin, Ernest J. Miller, Ruth Pointer, Albert Robinson, D. Shacklock, Aubrey Stevenson, Mervyn Walters, Brian C.J. Williams, Mary Wortley.

For their skill and advice we thank:
The photographic unit of Leicestershire County Record Office, Keith Thompson of Loughborough College of Art and Design.